THE SERIOUS BUSINESS OWNER'S GUIDE TO

CREATING CLIENTS FOR LIFE

SECRETS FOR LIFELONG RELATIONSHIPS

JIM CONNELLY & NINA HERSHBERGER

DEDICATION

To our supportive spouses:
Kate Connelly and Eldon
Hershberger. Without either of
you this book would not have
been written and we certainly
would never have been able to
do what we do.

Table of Contents

FOREWORD

I first met Jim Connelly when I was working at the University of Notre Dame. It took about three seconds to realize during that first meeting that I had met someone extraordinary. We met many times after that and I began to hear the stories that defined this remarkable man.

His father was an acute alcoholic and regularly chose  to take his aggression out on his son. From an early age, Jim had to earn money just to help support the family. He joined the work force and began his career delivering newspapers at age 7 and by age 10, if anyone in his home town of Turtle Creek, Pennsylvania wanted to buy a newspaper, he would buy it from Jimmy Connelly. Jim's entrepreneurial spirit had taken over by that time and he had 2 other boys working for him to deliver papers all over town.

Jim at age 10 – already an

A terrible student by his own admission, with poor reading, spelling and math skills, his teachers counseled him to quit school and get a job because they believed he wouldn't amount to anything.

However, through perseverance, he did finish high

Lou Holtz with Jim and Nina in East Liverpool, Ohio. Lou has been a great inspiration to them both.

school, albeit in 5 years, and went to the military to keep from being sent to jail for fighting.

When he returned home from the service, he once again found himself in front of a judge after a fight, but by then, Jimmy Connelly had made the biggest decision of his life – to leave Turtle Creek for California. The judge gave him one more chance and Jim left home the next morning for sunny California.

By the time I met him in 2004, his life journey had taken him around the world. Going from Turtle Creek High school to the General Manager of the Beverly Wilshire Hotel in 6 years was an incredible accomplishment for anyone, regardless of education. However, it didn't stop there. He went on to accomplish more than most people in life. Yet, the real measure of a man is their attitude and how much they give back.

As a business development expert, he mentored a young woman named Donna Jones and coached her from 13th place to Kodak's top sales position. However at the height of her career, a traumatic head injury accident left her in a comma for 48 days.

The medical community and her family had little hope of her returning to a normal life and thought she would do best in an institution in Connecticut. Jim, living in California at the time, asked for permission to care for and work with Donna for one year to see if he could make a difference in her recovery. That was 24 years ago. Today Donna lives a full and happy life. She lives independently, travels, runs in 10K races, and teaches English to Hispanic children. None of this would have happened if Jim Connelly had not decided to see if the impossible were possible. He wrote a best selling book, *One More Sunset*, about her remarkable recovery.

Several years after we met, with my marketing background and his business development expertise, we decided to go into business together and I left the University.

Frequently all it takes is someone from the outside to come in and look at the business with fresh eyes. As an "outsider" we see things that people working day-to-day overlook or simply get "used to". We use proprietary methods to uncover hidden assets in any business and turn those assets into a goldmine.

We add the greatest profit in the shortest time with the least amount of effort with the least amount of capital.

Jim and I wrote this book, not as the definitive textbook on how to succeed, but as a beginning guide on the path toward success.

Nina Hershberger

INTRODUCTION

When we set out to write this book, our challenge was to put in writing 70+ years of combined experience and wisdom that would answer this question:

What is our secret to success?

For Jim the question is usually phrased *How did you go from Turtle Creek with no money, no education, no connections and become the General Manager of a $100 million dollar hotel in 6 years? What's your secret?*

For Nina the questions is *How do you repeatedly make so much money for your clients with very little out of pocket expenses, even in tough economic times? What are your secrets?*

Actually, the answer is quite simple for both of us:

Create Customers For Life!

If your building and employees are gone tomorrow, but you still have your customer list, you can start again.

That list is golden!

Treat it like the precious commodity it is.

It is astonishing to us when we encounter

businesses people who don't have a list of their customers, haven't personally communicated with them ever (or at least for a long time), and basically ignore them in the never ending quest to find new customers.

If you learn nothing more from this book, learn this:

It's All About the Customer!

Jim: *"One night I got into a fight with an officer of the law. The fight wasn't an accident as fighting seemed to be a favorite pastime in Turtle Creek. What was accidental was that I was fighting a sheriff and didn't know it because he wasn't in uniform.*

My mother always said nothing good happens after midnight, so I shouldn't have been surprised that when the fight broke up I was thrown into jail (since it was way after midnight.)

The next day I was brought before a judge. It wasn't the first time and knowing myself, it probably wouldn't be the last time. I knew I could be spending the rest of my life in jail unless I did something different.

Jim's need to achieve made him determined to do a 1- arm handstand on a bet.

I promised the judge if he let me go that he wouldn't see me again because I would be leaving for California in the morning. For some reason he gave me one more chance and, true to my word, I paid an unemployed friend $100 to drive me to Beverly Hills, CA."

What Do You Want "More Of" In Your Business?

If someone could wave a magic wand and had the power to give you anything you wanted in your business, what one thing would you want?

Would it be?
→ More, better qualified prospects
→ Closing more sales or handling objections more effectively
→ More repeat business
→ What if your current customers felt that you were the only person in business who understood and could effectively serve their specialized, unique and individual needs and kept giving you more and more business? Would that be a magic wand answer?
→ Or, how about referrals? Take the best customer you have right now. How would you like to have more clients just like them? More than you could possibly handle?

→ Or maybe you just want your operations to run smoother with fewer mistakes, with happier more productive employees who say the right things to customers.

The truth is there's not any *one* thing that's more important than the other.

To succeed in business you must have a goal and a plan for each of these areas

In the chapters to follow, you're going to find out the real answers to keeping customers for life, not the text book answers - answers that have been tested and proven over the course of our 70+ combined years in business and marketing.

My first job in California

Jim: *"Shortly after I arrived in California, I found a job cleaning machinery for an aircraft parts manufacturer in Burbank, making $1.87 per hour. Being a street fighter all my life, I had a real need to achieve. I had a bad attitude, but a good work ethic.*

It didn't take me long to figure out that if I cleaned the machines while they were running, I could clean more machines than anyone else. I did this for three months until one day the edge of my sleeve got caught in one of the augers and almost made mincemeat out of me. That was the day I realized that job was not for me. I would loose an arm as surely as the sun rose every morning. That day I saw an ad in the Los Angeles Times:

ROOM CLERK WANTED.
EXPERIENCED ONLY.

Little did I know that on this day, my life would change forever."

Nina: *"Unlike Jim, I grew up in a very stable, loving home. My marketing and sales career began early when my mother said I begged her to let me go door to door selling rusty bobby pins. I don't remember that, but I certainly remember going door to door selling Christmas Cards. My grandmother owned a mimeo letter shop and when I was in elementary school, I would spend time in the shop putting labels on letters. Direct mail was in my blood even back then.*

Increasing Your Effectiveness

It's no secret that things are changing faster than ever before. Technology is more sophisticated, competition more keen, and consumers - the people who buy your products and services - are more educated, savvy and resourceful.

In a few minutes using a search engine on the internet, it is possible for your customers and your prospects to compare you to any number of competitors world wide.

If you're really going to be effective and successful

in the marketplace today, it is vital that you continually change, improve, adjust and up date your selling, service, and problem solving skills, as well as your methods of marketing and general business operation. It has been said:

> *People don't care how much you know,*
> *until they know how much you care.*

A room clerk who can't type?

Jim: *"The ad was for an experienced room clerk at the Beverly Wilshire Hotel on Rodeo Drive in Beverly Hills. If you've ever watched the movie Pretty Woman, you've seen the hotel.*

I don't know what made me decide I was qualified for that job since I couldn't spell or type, but I decided to apply anyway and I did everything wrong. I went at the wrong time. I wore the wrong clothes. Even my speech said I was the wrong guy.

But the moment I stepped through that front door and onto that thick red carpet, the hair on the back of my neck stood up. This was ME! I was home!

I had no idea where that feeling came from, but I knew I would do anything to get and keep a job at that hotel."

Feel the Fear and Do it Anyway

Besides working with our private clients, we also regularly hold CEO Masterminds in South Bend, IN. In Napoleon Hill's book, *Think and Grow Rich*, he identified being part of a Mastermind as one of the 17 critical principles for success. Mr. Hill defines the Mastermind principle as "an alliance of two or more minds working in perfect harmony for the attainment of a common goal." The Mastermind can be informal and loosely organized or it can be purposeful and structured to produce the greatest benefit.

In each of these Masterminds, two critical areas we address are

- How to Overcome Your Fears
- Taking Focused Action

Now, it is all relative but no one will ever know the gripping fear Jim experienced when he walked through the front door of the Beverly Wilshire Hotel. Everyone has fears and insecurities but to succeed in life, you must go through that door. Feel the fear, but go through anyway.

Where's Mr. Allen's office at?

Jim: *"I knew from the ad that I needed to see Mr. Allen. It was 5:00 p.m. and I hoped he would still be there. I walked up to the counter and asked for Mr. Allen. A bushy eye-browed man with a thick German accent named Mr. Kurt looked down at me and said his office was on the Mezzanine.*

Now, in Turtle Creek we didn't have mezzanines and I had no clue where that was. I headed towards the elevator and asked the woman running the elevator where Mr. Allen's office was at. 'Ah,' 'Pittsburgh" she said. The preposition at the end of the sentence had given me away; but she was kind and took me up to the Mezzanine, pointed in the direction of Mr. Allen's office and then turned and ran back to her post.

The Business You're In

If you don't learn another thing from our time together, remember this…

You're NOT in the (name your type of business) business…

You're in the PEOPLE business.

Read those sentences again and again and again. Digest them. Understand them. Internalize them. Make them an integral part of your business philosophy. Unless and until you do, your business will be no better and no different than any of your competitors.

You're hired!

Jim: *"Even though 5:00pm is not the best time to apply for a job, in my case it worked out. By that time, Mr. Allen's secretary had left for the day and he was in his office with no one to stop me from entering.*

I walked in and told him I was there to apply for the room clerk's job I saw in the paper. We talked and when he found out I had worked one summer for my uncle who owned a small hotel in Weed, California, he hired me on the spot. I was to report to Mr. Kurt. It was mine. I had the job. Now I had to find a way to keep it."

Let me explain about being in the "people business" by using the insurance profession as an example. As I do, think about how these principles might apply to your business.

Consider the way most people shop for auto insurance. They call up a number of insurance companies and ask for a quote. The agent asks what coverage the caller is currently carrying, and gives a quote based on those figures.

The caller thanks the agent then goes to the next number on their list. They keep repeating this scenario until they're convinced that they've found the lowest price. Usually, whichever company comes in lowest gets the business.

Wait a minute. Isn't there more to buying insurance than just 'low price'? Of course there is. Price is very important and it carries a lot of weight in a prospect's buying decision. But it's only one of many factors a person needs to consider when making a buying decision.

In actuality, there's very little difference in policies issued by any number of insurance companies in the same geographical area.

Likewise, there's usually very little difference in the products or services you sell versus those same types of products or services sold by your competitors.

General overhead costs, utilities, phones, supplies, wages, and product costs are also similar for most companies that sell like products and services.

So, if all those factors are pretty much the same, the prices charged by each individual business must, out of necessity, be fairly close as well.

It's true that one company may, for example, obtain a lower purchase price on their products and, as a result, be able to offer a more attractive sales price for a certain period of time. Eventually, however, things change and the playing field levels off once again. The point is that no matter what business you're in…

You will never maintain a long-term competitive advantage because of the products you offer, or... the prices you charge.

As soon as you develop a new product or offer a new service, it's just a matter of time before your competition latches on to it and offers the exact same thing. Maybe they even enhance it and offer it for a lower price. Then as soon as you lower your prices, your competition can do the same thing.

The marketplace in which you operate is so fiercely competitive, so cutthroat, so unforgiving, that...

you absolutely must do something to differentiate yourself from your competition!

If you don't, you'll be relegated to just another "me-too" business, just like all your competitors.

Now, you want to know the good news?

That's how your competitors operate... in a "ME-TOO!" mode.

Just look around. They're all the same. Their businesses all look the same. Their products are all the same. Even their advertising looks alike and says the same things as the next guy's. Because they all operate that way and don't know how or don't want to change, it gives you a tremendous opportunity!

Nina: *"One of our Mastermind members is the marketing genius behind a company that puts a vinyl "skin" on outdoor decks. Since all elevated outdoor decks will eventually leak, this is a very specialized business, but has a lot of competition. He recommended that they rise above the competition and immediately double their prices – putting them far above anyone else's price. He then created a video based website where the company owner recorded a video for each of the top 20 questions he gets about the deck covers.*

His passion, his believability came through loud and clear. There were no prices on the website.

Their sales skyrocketed.

Price was taken out of the equation.

All during the poor 2009 economy."

You see, if you keep doing what you've always done, you'll NOT keep getting what you've always gotten. You'll go backwards!

Quite frankly, there are companies right now meeting and planning strategies to take your market share away from you.

If you keep doing what you've always done – your competition will steal your customers and you'll soon be out of business!

But you… if you want to get something different… you've got to be willing to make some changes. And that's what we're all about. Making changes… changes that will produce real and measurable results in your business.

But, what you'll learn here isn't enough. These ideas and strategies alone won't work. You've got to take action on them if you expect anything different than what you're currently getting.

So, make the action commitment now… and let's get started!

Jim: *"I was the new Room Clerk for the Beverly Wilshire Hotel. That meant I had to type up the folios for the guests checking into the hotel, but I couldn't type and I couldn't spell. How was I going to make it?*

It was then I learned an important lesson in life. If you can't do it yourself, find someone who can help you – and quick. Never be afraid to ask for help.

Kay was a File Clerk at the hotel. She was from London and had a solid European work ethic. When my one-finger hunt and peck typing couldn't keep up, I'd ask her if she would help me. I paid her out of my own pocket and this went on for several months. She had one of the busiest jobs there but she still found time to help me. She was kind to me and I never forgot her kindness, and to this day I have the utmost respect and empathy for the new person on the job. I remember how it felt and I always give words of encouragement when I can.

"Brain cells create ideas. Stress kills brain cells. Stress is not a good idea."

Richard Saunders, aka Poor Richard

CHAPTER 1

Achieving Outstanding Business Success

Personal Traits of Exceptional Performers

Earl Nightingale, the famous radio personality and producer of self improvement books and programs made his life's work studying successful people and how they achieved their successes. A friend, who had long admired Earl for his ideas and philosophy, once asked him for advice. *What, based on his vast experience and knowledge, would be the one thing that would help a person ensure success both in business as well as in their personal life?*

Earl told his friend, "You know, I have often thought about that very question. And after all the years and all the study, I've come to the conclusion that your success in life or in business, for that matter, can be boiled down to one thing –

> *Your rewards will always be in direct proportion to the amount of service you render*

"You only have to look around," he said. "The people who serve others prosper. The people who don't serve others do not prosper.

"The problem," he continued, "is that unsuccessful people either haven't learned that great secret, or they don't apply it.

"The successful people are the ones who develop the habits of doing the things that unsuccessful people don't do for one reason or another."

What Failures Don't Like to Do

Earl's comments hit his friend like a big hammer that night, as he realized how true they were. The more you serve your customers and help them satisfy their needs, the more you will prosper.

As a person in business, be it owner, manager, professional or entrepreneur, serving your customers' needs effectively means that you must do the things that unsuccessful business owners, managers, professionals, and entrepreneurs don't do - things that most of us don't like to do either.

- There is no doubt that it is frustrating to work long hours or on weekends and only have a couple of "shoppers" stop by or be stood up for an appointment someone made with you. It's difficult because you'd much rather be with your family or pursuing other interests.

- It's tough to make telephone calls, only to be met with hostile and rude people on the other end.
- It's discouraging to set goals, schedule interviews, explain the technical aspects and benefits of the products and services you provide, overcome customer's objections and misconceptions and go out of your way to give exceptional service, only to have your customer go elsewhere because they found the same product or service for a few dollars less.

Enough of these experiences can be discouraging for anyone, and after a while, some people just quit trying. *They find it easier to adjust their standard of living downward to match their income, rather than to adjust their income upward to create their desired standard of living.*

Outstanding success is unusual and is dependent on many different factors.

Let's explore some success principles, the importance of a well-developed and executed plan and what personal traits and characteristics can help move you towards your goals more quickly:

Eight Personal Qualities for Success

1. Know What You Want

Know yourself and exactly what you want and expect out of your business. So many people enter into business and spend years without having any idea of what they want or what is possible to get out of their business.

In fact most business owners are working so hard *in* their businesses that they don't have time to work *on* them. As a result, they've become slaves to their business. They've got things backwards. They're working for their business rather than their business working for them.

Take the time to carefully analyze where you've come from, where you are now, and what you want to accomplish in your business or career. Then begin to set some meaningful goals to help you accomplish your objectives.

Meaningful goals are an essential requirement for success. With goals, you have a target to aim for, a purpose for being, and a direction to travel. Without goals, it's easy to wander aimlessly, getting sidetracked with any little thing that comes along.

When you set your goals, think of the word, "SMART." Your goals should be:

- **S**pecific,
- **M**easurable,
- **A**ttainable,
- **R**ealistic, and
- **T**ime bound

2. The Ability to Focus

The second quality is the ability to focus. Many people hesitate to go into business because they think they lack the talents and abilities necessary to succeed. They look at others who are successful and think that they must have unique talents or capabilities. Quite often, however, they are really quite average.

The main difference is that the successful person has developed the ability to focus. A person of average intelligence, who is focused on a clearly identified and specific goal, will consistently outperform the brightest people who are not focused on anything specific.

Focused on a Goal

Jim: *"Mr. Kurt hadn't interviewed me and he wasn't particularly happy I had been hired by Mr. Allen without consulting him. To be sure I was fully aware of my low position at the hotel, he gave me a copy of the organizational chart and added my name at the very bottom.*

His message to me was clear.

What he didn't know was that he had just given me my roadmap. I taped that organizational chart to the foot of my bed and every night and every morning I looked at it, determined that within 10 years I would be at the top.

Through the years I would pencil in dates by people's

names when I thought I could pass them and write notes like 'slacker', 'no ambition' and would chart my progress up the organizational chart.

What he thought would defeat me became the very thing that crystallized my goal."

Nina: *"Whenever we begin to work with clients, the first thing we spend time on is identifying where they are right now (their baseline) and then host a "visioning day" where we focus on setting their measurable goals. We have goals for number of new customers, conversion percentages, referrals, transaction dollars and profit margins. By the time the day is over, they have a roadmap for the next year that is specific and attainable.*

3. Determine the Price You Will Pay

For everything in life, there is a price and it must be paid before you can realize the rewards.

In many instances, it takes great sacrifice.

Every successful person can tell you that their success was not accidental. It took hours, days, years of practice, refining techniques, making mistakes and then learning from.

Think of professional athletes. We usually only see them when they perform – at a game or in competitions. But for every hour you see them compete or perform, they spend on average, 30 hours in preparation - on the field, in the gym, at the track, on the golf course, at odd hours, day and night in all kinds of weather, whether they felt like it or not - to hone their skills and abilities.

It was the sacrifices they made that made the difference between being a good athlete and a great one.

The same concept of sacrifice applies to operating a successful business.

If you want to reap the great and abundant rewards your business can provide you, you're going to have to do some not-so-glamorous things at some not-so-convenient times.

That may mean long hours at the office away from home, more travel than you'd like, making and accepting phone calls at odd hours, rearranging personal plans, putting off vacations.

If you have a family, this may prove to be a hardship on you. However, if you are just starting out in business or want to increase your existing business or achieve some new goals, you may have to make many sacrifices.

Simply stated: if you are not willing to make the necessary sacrifices, then you can't expect to be as successful in business as someone who is willing to make those sacrifices.

Champions are made when no one is watching.

Six Years Without a Vacation

Jim: *"When I was hired as a Room Clerk at the Beverly Wilshire, I was driving a 1949 Mercury. Many won't remember this, but back then on warm days when the sun was out, the fuel line would expand and create what was called a 'vapor lock'. The car would not start until it cooled down.*

Since California boasts many warm sunny days, my car, more often than not, wouldn't start until the sun had gone down. I couldn't go anywhere at the end of my 7am-3pm shift.

With no place to go and no extra money, I wandered the streets of Beverly Hills, but the police stopped me on several occasions, asking what I was doing. I didn't have the money to eat out, so I went to the owner of the hotel and offered to work in other departments after my normal shift until 7:30 p.m. for free to learn the business.

Neither he nor any of the other employees ever knew the real reason was that my car wouldn't start and I couldn't go anywhere. Since I was there over the dinner hour, I would also get my dinner for free. Now I was learning all aspects of the hotel business and getting all my meals for free besides.

The other workers thought I must be spying on them. Why would anyone work in another department after their own shift unless they were trying to spy on someone?

It was 6 years before I ever took a vacation. While everyone else was going to the beach on their days off, I was working.

But in the end it paid off. I was the first one to buy a beach house.

Invest to Reap The Rewards

Nina: *"One year while I was working at Notre Dame I volunteered to do the marketing to sell computers to the 2,000 incoming freshman. It wasn't my job, but by that time I invested massive amounts*

Here's a picture of the small portion of the books, manuals, systems, kits, home study courses and "swipe files" I have in my personal collection.

of time learning the secrets of direct response marketing and was pretty confident in what I could do.

While others would go home at night and sit in front of the television, I would be reading books. While they went on vacation with their extra money, I spent tens of thousands of dollars buying information and learning materials from direct response marketers. While they relaxed I had been writing copy and testing to see what worked and what didn't and was going to seminars with other gifted marketers.

The most the computer store had ever sold during the freshman event was $300,000. With a very limited budget, the sales reached $900,000! They were thrilled and asked me to do it again the next year and actually wanted me to bring in more sales. The only problem was – there was no budget for the project that year.

hmmmm....bring in more than $900,000 but with no marketing budget? It was a challenge I couldn't resist.

I designed a direct mail piece that looked like a newspaper and I went out and sold ad space. That gave me the money to two just 2 mailings. The results: $1,300,000 in sales!

4. Personal Responsibility

You are totally responsible for the success of your business and your life. There are no excuses.

- There may be setbacks,
- economic downturns,
- or problems that affect your business.
- Your suppliers or vendors may discontinue making or providing your favorite products or services.
- They may change the way they do business with you
- or even merge with another company.

Economies change; corporate policies change; prospects don't buy from you and the weather is too hot or too cold.

While all these things definitely have an impact on you, the way you do business and the sales you make, it is important to realize that those things are beyond your control and it is up to you, and you alone, to accept responsibility for the success of your business.

No matter what difficulties or challenges you might encounter, rest assured there are many people who have had difficulties and challenges far greater than any you are ever likely to encounter. Yet somehow they manage to pull through. And you can do the same.

Here's a little credo that can help you. It contains just ten, two letter words:

If it is to be, it is up to me.

That simple one line sentence says it all. It places the responsibility exactly where it should be... *directly on your shoulders.*

5. Be Committed
- Make a total commitment to your success. Once you have made the decision to be in business, be in that business.
- Jump in with both feet. Don't let anything hold you back.
- Even more than getting in the business, is seeing that the business gets in you.
- Make a commitment that you are going to succeed, no matter what.
- Don't try to work two different jobs or projects at one time. You can't do either of them justice, and you'll likely end up frustrated and broke and never know whether or not you could have been successful.

Never Give Up

Jim: *In 1987 my wife and I were at Notre Dame picking out the carpet and paint colors for the condo we had bought at the edge of campus. It was a cold February, snowy night in South Bend and the smart people were home staying warm. We were the only guests in a local restaurant for awhile until the builder of our condo complex came in with a young man." Jim," he said. "I have someone I'd like you to meet."*

They joined us for dinner and the young man began to tell us his story. When he was finished I pounded my fist on the table and said "This should be a movie!" From under the table he brought out a folder which held the screenplay of his story.

"Rudy", I said. "You can't make a movie in South Bend. Come stay with us in California and let's see if we can help you get to the right people." He came and stayed with us in our home and we sent him in our limo to the different studios for appointments with the studio heads.

One connection led to another and another and the rest is history. The movie 'Rudy' is now a classic and one of the most popular movies of all time.

As a football player, Rudy was not unique. There were many men who had walked on to the Notre Dame Football program. Over the years many have had success and played much more than Rudy. Rudy played for only 27 seconds but he turned that moment into an entire career. Rudy was the one who never gave up on his dream to see it made into a movie.

6. The Extra Mile

The sixth personal quality necessary to achieve outstanding success in business is the willingness to go that extra mile.

It's the "Under promise, over deliver" concept, and can be summed up in the following statement:

"If you are always willing to do more than what you get paid for, the day will come when you will be paid for more than what you actually do."

Jim: *"As I continued up the ladder at the hotel, the controller Jacque LeVeque, took a special interest in me. He could see I had a great work ethic and he thought I was a nice young man. One day he pulled me aside and said he wanted to put me on a reading program. Up to that point, the only book I had even started (but never finished) was Tom Sawyer. I had never read a book completely through.*

Besides telling me to start reading the New York Times and the Wall Street Journal he gave me a list of 3 books:

1. *Think and Grow Rich by* Napoleon Hill,
2. *Psycho-cybernetics by* Maxwell Maltz
3. *How to Win Friends and Influence People by* Dale Carnegie.

These books became my best friends – especially Think and Grow Rich. Dr. Hill wrote it in 1937, the year I was born, and I say he wrote it for me.

One of the 17 principles he identified all successful people possessed was 'going the extra mile'. Here's what he said:

'Render more and better service than that for which you are paid, and sooner or later you will receive compound interest on compound interest from your investment. For it is inevitable that every seed of useful service you sow will multiply itself and come back to you in overwhelming abundance.'

There's no traffic jam on the extra mile.

7. Control Your Time

The seventh quality is that you must master and take control of your time. Each one of us has the same 24 hours in each day. When those hours are gone, they cannot be replaced. They are gone forever, never to be recaptured.

You must treat your time as a precious commodity and guard it wisely and selfishly. Don't let anyone disrupt you or take you away from the focus you have on your goals.

People who don't have goals are used by people who do. If you let others draw you away from your goals, you are simply saying that their goals are more important than your own.

If you are serious about business success – really serious, then this is one of the most important and critical areas to defend.

Be especially careful how much television you watch and web surfing you do. **Leaders are readers.** If you let the hours slip by in front of a screen, you cheat yourself.

8. Persistence and Determination

Develop persistence and determination. From time to time you will encounter set backs or reach plateaus where it seems like nothing is going right.

Your competitors lower their prices, run massive ad campaigns and unheard of promotions and the next thing you know, your customers and clients begin doing business with them.

Business is walking out the back door faster than it's coming in the front door. Your volume is beginning to drop and you become concerned.

You seem to be spending more time in a defensive posture than you do in servicing your existing customers, and you're losing.

Now is not the time to give up. Now is the time to dig in and begin to play offensively. Be determined not to lose your good customers – the ones you worked so hard to get. Your strategy should be to keep in touch with them and continue providing exceptional service.

Nearly every business is cyclical. Eventually things will change. While you can't be competitive on price all the time, you can be competitive on the service you give and the empathy you have for your customers and their problems.

Remember, action is the key. As we discussed earlier, it's not what you know; it's not what you talk about; it's what you do. True success in business or in life is an ongoing process

The Road to Success is Always Under Construction.

Some say that knowledge is power, but knowledge isn't power unless it's applied. This chapter has supplied you with some vital knowledge necessary to be successful in business. You now have the knowledge – now it's up to you to put that knowledge into action.

Jim: *There were many more people at the Beverly Wilshire with more knowledge and education than me. What they didn't have was the passion and commitment to climb the ladder.*

I felt no pain in working 14 hours a day for 6 years without a vacation. I had a clearly defined goal and knew I had to outsmart the most educated ones working there. I applied all the principles of Napoleon Hill's philosophy to overtake the best and the brightest to become the youngest General Manager in the Hotel's history.

"Laughter is the shortest distance between two people."

Victor Borge

CHAPTER
2

How Do Your Customers See You?

Establishing A Positive Identity In The Minds Of Your Customers

Think of the word, "Professional." What image comes to your mind? Do you visualize a doctor, a dentist, a lawyer, or perhaps the president of a large corporation? Do you see yourself?

What criteria do you use to define a "professional?"

What about your customers, for example? How do you think they define a "professional?" Are you a "professional" in their eyes?

The way you run your business and handle your customers' needs on a daily basis says a lot about you and the position you occupy in their minds.

In truth, your occupation should be viewed as being just as "professional" as doctors, dentists, lawyers, or any other type of business head.

The critical question is how professionally do you perform within the scope of your occupation?

While this program is not a sales training course,

it's important to know that no matter what your role in business is, you're involved in sales in one form or another.

And if you have staff or employees who are involved in sales, it's important for you to know the following information.

Five Types Of Salespeople

Just as different salespeople have their own unique personalities, they also have different skill levels when it comes to selling and servicing their customers.

As we discuss the various types of salespeople and classify them according to their skill level, you will no doubt recognize some of the people you know or have encountered in the past. As we do, take an honest look at yourself to see where you might fit.

Professional Visitor

This person doesn't have any problem making appointments. In fact, they thrive on it. They enjoy talking to people and getting to know them, and may even engage in a casual discussion of their customers' needs and problems.

Their conversation with a customer or prospect may or may not eventually involve the subject of how their products or services can benefit the buyers, and if it does, it usually has to be instigated by the customer or prospect.

A typical sales presentation will be oral, with

very little, if any, use of visual materials, product brochures, or printed proposals.

Order Taker

These people don't mind talking to customers, clients or prospects if they don't have to initiate the call. They are uncomfort¬able making appointments and would rather have the customer or prospect come to them.

If the phone rings, they'll take the call and even discuss the customer's needs. But it's tough for them to pick up the phone and dial a customer's number.

They operate best from a base of "low price," and have difficulty handling objections. They would rather wait until someone asks for something specific, then they have no trouble filling the order.

Peddler

These are "sales oriented" people. They have good product knowledge, but lack in people skills. They operate from a sort of "hit and run" approach.

This person will assume a certain level of product knowledge on the part of the customer, and spend very little time establishing rapport with them. These people are either "product oriented," or "price-oriented." Their entire presentation is based on product features or price, with little regard as to how the product or service will benefit the customer.

The Peddler is the most prevalent type of salesperson you will find. Telemarketers who work the consumer market fit into this category.

With the new "DO NOT CALL" regulations, it doesn't happen as often now with incoming calls. However, if you've ever tried to order anything over the phone from TV advertisements, then you know how frustrating and time consuming it can be. All you want to order is that one item but the telemarketer doesn't hear you and they just march right over you. They tell you non-stop all about the dozen other wonderful products that you are entitled to buy at this once-in-a-lifetime discounted rate. Talk about disregard for the customer.

This inconvenience and non-listening mode is most aggravating. In these types of calls, the salesperson shows no concern for the prospect's time, present level of product knowledge, or whether or not there's any level of need, want or desire to know more about what they're selling. For them it is a numbers game.

This type of approach is an insult to the prospect or customer, and is one of the biggest mistakes a salesperson can make.

Problem Solver

These are salespeople who enjoy getting in front of people, ferreting out problems, needs and wants, and discussing workable solutions. They have empathy for the customer, can see the customer's needs from the customer's point of view, and enjoy helping the customer solve their problems.

The problem solving person is good at establishing rapport with the prospect or customer. They identify their needs, wants and desires, developing creative proposals and making effective presentations.

But when it comes time to ask for the order or close the sale, they tense up, lose their confidence, or otherwise fail to close the sale. Their customers or prospects, now having their needs identified and solutions presented, go elsewhere looking for a "better buy."

This salesperson has done all the work and an Order Taker for another company gets the sale – and the commission. After the Peddler, this is the next most common type of salesperson.

Counselor

In the business world, it's not uncommon for companies to have a staff of lawyers or legal counsel on retainer to give advice.

The Counselor knows that when it comes to important buying decisions, his or her customers, be they companies, corporations, or individuals, should have the same expert advice available.

To the Counselor, buying any type of product or service is a serious matter and can be an important tool for solving a need, satisfying a problem or adding to their profits, convenience or lifestyle.

They know that their customers need professional and qualified representation and advice, and the Counselor will do whatever it takes to provide it for them.

Like corporate legal counsel, this salesperson

postures him or herself as being "on retainer," always available to give advice on matters pertaining to the products or services they sell. They make it clear in the customer's mind that there is absolutely no need for them to go anywhere else for answers.

The Counselor knows how to establish rapport, build professional trust and credibility, identify their customers' current prob¬lems, develop effective proposals, and offer credible and workable solutions. They make their presentation in such a way that their customers have no question in their minds but that they must buy the concepts they present, and hence, the product or service.

In addition, they have the ability to point out other potential problems that the customer might encounter and help them solve those needs as well.

Salespeople who function at this skill level carefully review the customer's needs, both stated and unstated, and skillfully set in motion a plan to address those needs now, or at a later date.

Objections rarely come up because the Counselor has taken the time to anticipate what objections may arise, and then build the answers to the potential objections into his or her presentation.

This salesperson will get every drop of business the customer has, not because of price, but because the customer knows the salesperson really cares about them, understands their needs, and is willing to take the time to identify those needs and offer workable and credible solutions.

Jim: *"While learning the hotel business as a Room Clerk, I imagined that each and every one of our guests wore a sign around their neck that silently shouted:*

MAKE ME FEEL IMPORTANT!

How Do Your Customers See You?

How do you think your customers see you?

- Are you someone they might classify as a "typical salesperson"?
- Are you someone who is more interested in selling them another product or service just to receive a commission instead of really evaluating the customers' needs?
- Or do your customers and prospects view you more as a counselor? Are you someone they like and can relate to and who is genuinely interested in them? Do you make sure they have the right product for their individual and specific needs, at the best possible price? If there is a problem will you work together to make things right?

How you answer these basic and important questions is critical to your success in business. It can mean the difference between enormous success, mediocrity, or even dismal failure

- If your customers welcome you as a counselor or advisor,
- someone with their best interests in mind,
- who can help them identify and solve their problems,
- They will feel good about you.
- They will welcome your calls and look forward to spending time with you.
- You will be viewed as professional and confident.

Consequently, you will feel good about yourself, and the role you play relative to your customer. As you fill the role of problem solver, you can't help but reinforce and strengthen that positive image in both you, and your customer's minds.

What Your Customers Really Want

As a business person, it is important for you to understand that *only 35% of the reason people buy the products or services you offer is for the actual product or service itself.*

The other *65% of the reason they buy is for what YOU can do or provide for your customer beyond the product or service.*

In other words, if you are trying to sell your customers and prospects *products and services*, you are wasting your time. They are only 35% interested in *products and services*.

But they are 65% interested in the benefits of <u>having you involved</u>.

You see, chances are good that your customers and prospects can buy the same or comparable product or service from any one of several of your competitors. And with that product or service, your competitor may offer a number of additional advantages, as well.

They may have a lower price, better quality product, some added bonuses or extra services, a location that's more convenient, or a payment plan that fits their budget better.

In today's tough market, it's difficult to compete on price or product. You may have a certain advantage for a period time because you have a lower price than your competitors, but we all know that it will be short-lived.

The truth is, you will never be able to maintain a long-term competitive position in the marketplace because of the prices you charge or the products you provide.

It'll just be a matter of time before one of your competitors lowers their prices or duplicates (or even betters) your product, or you raise your prices because you no longer have the necessary margins to justify your prices.

But there's one thing your customers can't get from any of your competitors. And that's you, along with your empathy, problem solving expertise and the knowledge, education and commitment to service that you bring to their specific and unique situation.

My Secret Filing System

Jim: *"As I continued to climb the hotel ladder I never let go of the job I just left. I would do my new job plus the ones I had left behind. I worked harder and longer hours juggling all the details.*

I knew that every person who stayed at our hotel had a choice to stay with us or go somewhere else. It was my job to make sure that all our clients, including the Hollywood stars, presidents, and captains of industry, all considered our hotel their number 1 choice.

I knew how to make someone feel special. I paid attention to what they liked and what their passion was. I would watch what they drank, what they ate, knew what their favorite color was and the subjects they liked to talk about. I'd then go back to my office and write copious notes on 3x5 cards on each of our regular guests. That was back before computers and even credit cards.

I knew what color carpet they liked, what side of the hotel they preferred to face, if they drank wine or scotch. So the next time they came to the hotel, I would greet them and tell them we had their favorite room

waiting for them and when they entered the room, their favorite drink and fresh fruit were waiting.
I knew what they wanted and made sure they always got it.

"Do what you say you're going to do, when you say you're going to do it, in the manner it should be done."
Jim Connelly

How Much Are You Worth?

Strategies for Determining and Increasing Your Value to Your Customers

You are in business for yourself. You may own your own business, or you may be associated with another company or firm. You may be an employee, a partner or an independent contractor. Your working agreement or arrangement doesn't really matter.

Just consider yourself as a business that prospers or falters financially by the amount of commission dollars you generate. The point is, even though you may be working for or associated with another company, you are really working for yourself.

Three Keys for Success

It's important to realize that your success in business will always be determined by 3 things:

1. **The need or demand for what you do**
2. **Your ability to do it**
3. **The difficulty in replacing you.**

In other words, how valuable are you and the services you perform to other people?

To illustrate this point, let's apply our 3 step formula to the job of an elevator operator. In today's world of push button, self operated elevators, how much need is there for the services he or she performs?

It doesn't take much knowledge or training, so an operator can be replaced without much difficulty. As a result, elevator operators, if you can even find one, are not paid much.

Now, contrast the elevator operator and the money they command with that of a professional major league baseball player, specifically a player who is good at batting.

What is the *need for what they do?* A look at attendance figures for baseball games will give you the answer.

How about the batter's *ability to do what he does?* Sports analysts say that the action of hitting a ball moving towards you at over 90 miles per hour is the single most difficult movement in sports.

In the games of basketball, the target (the hoop) doesn't move. The same is true in golf. While the ball moves, the hole or goal remains stationary. In football, there are 11 teammates all with a common goal of advancing the ball. But in baseball, it's the batter alone trying to hit a small, 90 m.p.h. target with his bat. So it stands to reason then, that the better or more often a batter can hit the ball, the more he or she will be compensated.

Now, what about the *difficulty in replacing* a good batter? When only the best in the world can hit the target less than a third of the time, and most of the other players are successful far less than that, it doesn't take long to realize why the best batters are among the highest money makers in the world.

Obtaining Superior Rewards

You can tell exactly how valuable the service you perform is by how much people are willing to pay you for it. If you do the same job that everybody else does, and do it no better than the way they do it, you can't expect to earn more money, or be considered any more valuable than those other people.

In other words, you will be rewarded in direct proportion to the value you provide your customers.

Now, if the products and services you sell or provide are similar in coverage and price to everyone else's, then the difference between you and other people in your position has to be in the type and amount of personal service you provide your clients.

Personal service, then, has to be the area you excel in. It becomes your competitive edge.

Guaranteeing Business Success

One of the main keys to success in business is to make sure, first and foremost, that there is a great *need or demand for what you do*

One of the best ways to guarantee that is to make sure you only spend your time selling to qualified prospects, i.e. people who need, want and can pay for what you're selling. There may be people who need or want what you have, but if they can't afford to pay for it, you'll spend endless amounts of time and energy and get nowhere.

On the other hand, there may be people who have the ability to pay, but not have the need or want. In these cases, you can also waste considerable time and chances are no sale will result from your efforts.

The second point is that you are paid in direct proportion to your *ability to do what it is that you do* - that is, identify, qualify and sell the products and services you offer to your prospects and customers, and then service their needs as they arise.

In some businesses, the sole function of salespeople is to seek out qualified prospects and sell them the products or services offered by the business. The necessary service work for the customer is provided by an office or support staff.

In other businesses, each salesperson is responsible in every way for each of their customer's needs, from the initial sale, to providing all the necessary service the customer might require, including updating the product or service, customer complaints, changes of address, or any other service work that may be needed.

The determining factor then, is not what your responsibilities are, but rather, how good you are at performing those responsibilities.

Third, remember, that you are paid in direct proportion to the difficulty *in replacing you.*

When I think of this area, I think of Disneyland and Disneyworld. As attractions go, they have very little competition. And as far as theme parks? They are unsurpassed.

Why? Because they have met the criteria outlined in the 3 step formula.

Let's consider each of the steps of the formula as they apply to Disney.

First, is there a need for what they do? Certainly there must be. Entertainment is the largest business in the world today, both in terms of participants and in total dollar revenue.

Next, how about Disney's ability to do what they do? With over 53 million people visiting their 3 parks each year, evidence would indicate that they are doing a whole lot of things right.

And finally, the difficulty in replacing them? Nothing has come close yet, and with those 53 million people spending over $3 billion, odds are that the people who visit the Disney properties are pretty satisfied and will visit again.

The Law of Unlimited Abundance

Walt Disney was a man of extraordinary vision and foresight. He knew what it would take to be successful in his chosen area of business. He developed a formula that expressed his philosophy and could be used in any type of business to ensure its success. He called it his "Law of Unlimited Abundance."

Walt said it didn't matter what type of business or endeavor a person was engaged in, they could be successful and enjoy *unlimited abundance*, if they would simply follow his formula.

Walt Disney's "Law of Unlimited Abundance," stated that to be successful, you must

"Do what you do so well that the people who see you do it, will want to see you do it again, and will bring others to see you do it."

That's the credo that built the enormous successes of Disneyland and Disneyworld and in their arena of operation, they stand alone.

Disney's Law Can
Work For You!

It can be similar in your business world, too. You
see, the key is to *do what you do,* not what someone
else does, but what *you* do. You don't have to copy.
You simply do your job the way only you can. That's
what makes you special, sets you apart from others,
and attracts people to you.

Then you do what you do *so well,* that is, provide
the type of service your customers require, want, or
need in an exceptional manner, that it leaves no room
for mediocrity.

And if you will do that so, *the people who see you
do it,* (your customers), *will want to see you do it
again,* (that's repeat business), *and will bring others
to see you do it,* (that's referral business), you too, can
meet with an unparalleled success.

Because so few people perform in business
that way, it sets you completely apart from all the
competition. Customers can't get the kind of service
you offer from anyone or anywhere else. It's simply
not available anywhere, at any price.

So, by default, you become unique, different, and
difficult to replace. And it will be reflected in your
business and your income. It has to. There's no choice.
It is a basic, eternal law of nature. You simply reap the
results of what you've sown.

You Reap What You Sow

Jim: *"I was fortunate to be at the Beverly Wilshire Hotel when Walt Disney was one of our stockholders. I believed in his philosophy and used it to provide the best service for all our guests, especially our daily VIPs. (Remember my filing system?)*

The proof was in the results of my efforts to be the best. The president of MGM Studios, who was a frequent guest at our hotel, mandated that all MGM movie stars under contract would stay at the Beverly Wilshire Hotel when in Southern California. Some of those included Elvis Presley, Lauren Bacall, Liz Taylor, Richard Burton, Julie Christie, Warren Beatty and many others.

The Customer Signs Your Paycheck

It really is the customer who signs your paycheck. And although you must see that your company's interests are always considered, you must not lose sight that the customer is the boss.

They are the whole reason your job exists in the first place. They hire you to help them make good personal and business decisions. They trust you to help them see that their problems or needs are solved or satisfied in an efficient and cost-effective manner, and they pay you well to do your job. It is the wants, needs and desires of your customers that should determine all of your business activity.

Develop a Customer/Prospect List

Find Out What They Want

Give Them What They Want

"Control your destiny or someone else will."
Jack Welch

Why People Buy

Identifying Basic Buying Motives

People don't buy for the sake of owning a certain product or service. Rather, they buy because of the benefits they will receive as a result of owning that product or service.

Example: in one year, 250,000 quarter inch drills were sold, and not one person who bought a drill wanted a quarter inch drill. Instead, they bought the drills because they wanted the benefits the drill could provide - a hole.

People Buy for the Benefits

Like the quarter inch drills, people are not interested in products, but they are interested in the benefits the products will provide them. It makes sense then, that when you are making a presentation, you don't emphasize *products*.

Rather, you should talk in terms of *specific benefits* and how those benefits apply directly to the particular prospect in front of you at the time.

If you try to sell them for any reason other than their own, you run the risk of alienating them. This usually ends up destroying the sale you are trying to make, as well as any future sales.

Trying to figure out why people make certain decisions can be a complicated, even frustrating process, at best. But an understanding of basic buying motives can make your job much easier.

Motives for Buying

Behavioral psychologists tell us there are seven basic motives that move a person to action – that cause them to buy. An understanding of these motives and how they apply to your customers and prospects at the time a buying decision is being made can give you a tremendous advantage.

1. Desire for Gain or Profit

Nobody likes to lose. People want something in return for their efforts and hard work. The easier they can get it, the better. The success of the lottery games in various states bears testimony to people trying to find an easy way to obtain gain and profit.

The products you sell can help your customers realize their dreams for gain or profit, too. Your customers can and will invest in various types of products or services you sell – not to own them, per se, but in an effort to increase their profitability and the amount and value of their assets. For example a grocery store might purchase a computer program, not because they want to own a new disk, but because it will help them track their inventory to see which items sell best, and stock up accordingly. Benefits.

2. Fear of Loss or Need For Security
People will go to great lengths to prevent from losing something. In an effort to protect their property, some people install burglar or fire alarms, smoke detectors, or night lights that automatically come on when movement is detected.

Some people carry spray cans of mace or tear gas, while others have resorted to carrying guns or other weapons to protect themselves. Psychologists say that the fear of loss or the need for security is perhaps the greatest of all the motives.

If the products and services you sell can help protect your clients, their families or their businesses from loss, or if you can in someway increase their security, you owe it to them to capitalize on that fact as much and as often as possible.

3. Pride of Ownership, Or Status
People want to be noticed and recognized. Children do it all the time – riding bicycles with no hands, climbing trees, putting on shows and shouting to their parents, "Look at me!"

Adults do the same things, but in different ways. While they may not verbally shout out, they still want the attention. "Look at me!" they silently shout.

They do it by the kinds of cars they drive, the

clothes and jewelry they wear, the houses they live in.

While people may buy because of the benefits, they like others to see the actual product. In some cases, it's just another way to say, "Look at me!"

4. Interest in Doing Something Easier or More Efficiently

We all want methods of doing things easier. A person only has to look around their home to notice the abundance of time and/or money saving conveniences we all enjoy.

What about your products or services?

Do they somehow make a person's job, or a business' way of doing things easier or more efficient?

And if they do, what are the direct and indirect benefits to your prospect or customer?

Is this something you can capitalize on?

5. The Desire for Excitement or Pleasure

Our bodies are hardwired for pleasure and excitement. From the youngest age, little babies love to be raised in the air; little kids get a great thrill from climbing, jumping and swinging; teens and tweens can't wait to spend a day at the amusement park; and adults have a whole range of pleasure seeking, excitement generating options. The point is, people are motivated by what makes them feel good.

For some people, feeling good comes with ownership. For others excitement and pleasure comes in the acquiring.

Think back about the times you set a goal and worked hard to achieve it and how excited you were in the process.

Sometimes it's not the end result that counts as much as the process of acquiring.

Of course, these applications have to do with "things." Some people really enjoy acquiring "things" and even keep score by how much they accumulate.

Other people gain great pleasure or excitement knowing that their family's educational and financial futures are secure.

Business owners or entrepreneurs, for example, like to know that their businesses are operating at peak efficiency and profitability. There is pleasure and pride in meeting the needs of their customers.

6. Self Improvement or an Increase in Effectiveness

The investment you make in reading this book is a good example of your desire for self improvement and increased effectiveness. People want and need to improve and to be able to do things more efficiently.

Sometimes that involves taking risks with time or money. Not all risks have to be "risky." Calculated risks based on well thought-out plans and outcomes are the safest way to go, and can contribute greatly to the successful improvement in effectiveness and efficiency.

Attending seminars, reading books, joining a Master Mind group – all of these activities will increase your knowledge and expertise in your field.

7. The Desire for Importance and The Need To Feel Appreciated

According to noted psychiatrist Dr. Abraham Maslow, to be accepted and appreciated is one of the basic needs of all humans. Children want to be accepted by their parents and peers, and parents want their children to remember and appreciate them when they grow up and leave home.

In his book, *The Human Side of Enterprise,* Douglas McGregor explains that while money is important, workers are motivated more by "significant works," and a feeling of being needed and appreciated.

People want to make a difference and be appreciated for it. Fathers and mothers not only have an obligation to see that their family's futures are provided for, they want their family to understand and appreciate their efforts as well.

Business owners have an obligation to the people who buy from them, the employees and their families who work for them, and the suppliers and the vendors who sell to them. Too often, each of those groups of people live with an attitude of expectancy and entitlement. That is, they expect that the business owner will take care of them. How much better it would be if more appreciation would be shown to those who make our lives better.

If the products or services you provide the marketplace can help make this possible, you may have an open ticket to success because of the great unsatisfied need that exists.

If you understand these basic motives and how they apply to your business of selling your products and services, and then sell to the needs (both stated and unstated) of your customers and prospects, you will prosper.

And if you are not prospering, it simply means you have not uncovered your prospects' and customers' motives for buying. You are not addressing their specific needs. In most cases you can't wait for your customers to tell you what they want. You have to be able to recognize or uncover their needs.

Remember, you are ultimately responsible for the success or failure of your business. If you are doing it right or wrong, either way, the marketplace will let you know.

The Loyalty of the Customer

Customers make an interesting study. It seems that they always want the very most for the very least. They are ruthless, selfish, demanding and disloyal.

You know the story. You've done business with someone for several years and they've been good customers. You've given them the best service possible and you think they are your customers for life. But then some little thing, possibly out of your control, goes wrong. Or maybe they see an ad or get a call from a competitor, with a slightly lower price, and the next thing you know, they are gone, oftentimes without a single word to you.

At first you don't notice it. But one day you realize that it's been a while since you've seen or heard from that customer. When you find out what happened, you feel badly because, if they would have just called you, you might have been able to make a couple of changes and save the business. But it's too late, they're gone.

This scenario is repeated time and again with businesses owners from every company, who sell every type of product or service. To pretend that couldn't happen to you, is simply deceiving yourself.

Don't let a customer get away. **You must continue to "romance them".**

One of the best ways to cut down on the loss of your good customers is to resell them on the reasons they bought from you in the first place. Regularly scheduled meetings or conversations with your customers to remind them of their motives can go a long way in helping insulate your business from the competition.

Remember that your competition has similar products, services and prices. Also remember that your customer's reasons for buying are only 35% based on those products, services, and prices. The other 65% is for what *you* can do for them.

Spend the time with them. Review their needs, wants and concerns. Remind them why they bought from you in the first place. Reinforce their motives and their decisions for buying and you will reduce your customer defection rate and develop not only loyal customers, but friends, as well.

"Show me a successful person and I guarantee you they have overcome adversity"

Lou Holtz

CHAPTER 5

The Main Purpose of Your Business

Getting and Keeping Customers - Profitability Is Number One Priority

When you have an effective system that will allow you to *profitably* get and keep *quality* customers who will return to do business with you again and again, and then actively and enthusiastically refer you to others, your business will produce more profits than you can possibly imagine.

On the other hand, if you don't have enough customers buying from you or using your services regularly, then you're not likely to stay in business for very long and will never have the chance to make a profit.

Now, let's take a minute and look closely at the individual components of this important business skill…

Knowing How to Profitably Attract Quality Customers

Customers are the lifeblood of any business. Without customers buying the products and services you have to offer, you wouldn't have a business to begin with. But customers alone aren't enough.

You want *quality* customers. You want customers who are pleasant to deal with; customers who return to repurchase from you again and again; customers to whom you can sell and realize a reasonable profit from.

And you want to be able to *profitably* attract them. In other words, the return you realize from your investment of advertising or marketing dollars to acquire new customers, should be positive. You want a positive R.O.I., or return on your investment.

Next, you want to…

Maximize their Financial Potential for Your Business

Each of your customers has certain needs and wants. The more of those needs and wants you can handle for them and the more benefits you can provide them, the more profits you'll realize.

It should be your goal to sell as many products and services to your customers as they need.

You should never take advantage of them or your relationship with them, but you should make every effort to sell them everything necessary for you to meet their needs.

To be frank, it really comes down to this. If you really do provide the best products and services in the marketplace, and if you really are the business who can serve your customers' needs better than anyone else (and if you're not, you either need to become that business or get out of the business), then you have a moral and an ethical responsibility to make sure that every one of your customers at least has the opportunity to take advantage of all that you offer.

And you should do everything in your power that's *reasonable* and *ethical* to give them that opportunity.

Next you want to…

Convert Your Customers to Advocates Who Actively and Enthusiastically Refer You to Others

By definition, an advocate is someone who is a backer, a supporter, a promoter, a believer, an activist, a campaigner, a sponsor.

The last thing you need is a database full of one-product, or one-service customers who buy the minimum amount from you, complain about your prices every time they make a purchase, and give the rest of their business to the company or business who has the lowest prices or a "better deal."

There's no way you can make a profit on these types of customers. Besides, they make your life miserable and drive you crazy in the process.

You want customers who not only give you all or the majority of their business, but re-buy from you year after year. You want customers who are so happy and so pleased with what you do for them that they actively and enthusiastically campaign for you.

You want to know that the story they tell about you is so compelling that the people they tell are nearly forced to call you and ask for your help. Those are the people who make your job fun, enjoyable and profitable.

And finally, you want to…

Keep Your Customers for Life

Reliable studies demonstrate that the more needs a business handles for a customer, the longer they can expect that customer to do business with them.
In the insurance business for instance, an agent increases his chances of keeping an insured for three years or more by the following percentages:

- 45% if the agent insures only the auto policies
- 50% if both the auto and homeowners policies are insured

- 60% with auto, homeowners and life policies, and
- **97% with auto, homeowners, life and health policies!**

While these figures are illustrative of the insurance business, the same principle is true of most other businesses. The idea is that by serving all the needs your prospects or customers have, with the products and services you provide or have access to, you lock yourself in and the competition out.

Obviously, the longer you retain your customers, the more chances you will have to sell them additional products and services, and the more referrals you can get from them. It all adds up to increased profits for you.

Retaining your customers, the ones you've spent so much time, effort and money attracting and convincing to do business with you, is critically important.

Studies suggest that it costs six times more to get a new prospect to buy from you than it does to get an existing customer to purchase from you again. And it's sixteen times easier to sell an existing customer than it is a new prospect.

When you add it all up, for every 5% increase in customer retention, you'll generate a 30% to 45% increase in profitability over an 18 month period.

Depending on the nature of the products and services you sell, if your re-purchase rate isn't in the high 90 percentile range, you have some work to do.

A lost customer is much more than just a lost customer and their attending profits. In future chapters we'll discuss how to determine what the actual cost of a lost customer is and what to do to prevent them from leaving.

But for now, just keep this important point in mind. If you're going to be successful in business, no matter what you sell, then you've got to have an intense focus on your customer. You've got to find out what they want and do everything you can to help them get it.

And if you want to make a fortune rather than just a living, you can't do it for only a few. You must do it for large numbers of people.

The success of your business will depend on how well you serve your customers… the people who buy from you!

> *"Keep your mind on the things you want*
> *and off the things you don't want."*
> Napoleon Hill

The Four Primary Ways to Grow Your Business

Maximizing the Return on Your Efforts in These Four Key Areas

One of the most important things for any business person to realize is that there are four *principal* ways to grow a business – any business.

1. Get More Customers

That's it. Build your customer base. Get more prospects to buy from you and become your customers.

You know how it works. When more people buy from you, you take in more gross dollars, and as a result (depending on your margins and overhead), you make more bottom line profits.

As a spin-off benefit, the more people you add to your customer base the larger it becomes, and the larger it becomes, the more people you have to go back to for additional sales and the referrals they're capable of giving you.

It's in this one single area where most business owners, including your competition spend most of their time, effort and money.

If you've been in business for any length of time, you probably realize that getting new customers is not always the easiest, the most time-efficient, or most profitable thing you can do.

Most businesses only have one or two main methods of attracting new prospects to their businesses.

Advertising is one. Big dollars are spent every year by many companies trying to get new customers and increase their market share.

It can be on a large scale reaching around the world or it can be on a small scale reaching within cities or even within neighborhoods.

It can be on television, radio, in print and now on the internet.

Each business, industry, or profession has their own methods to contact those who are most likely to be interested in their products and services.

Think about your business and your company for a minute. Chances are that you, like nearly every other business owner in your industry or profession, also utilizes one or two main methods of attracting new prospects.

Most likely, the method you use is the same method that nearly every other business uses. It's called the, *"That's how things are done in our industry or profession,"* method.

Typically, when a person first chooses to go into business they look around and see what everyone else is doing.

Then they layout their office, shop or place of business, just like every other similar type of business they've seen.

They look at what everyone else is doing to market or promote their businesses, products and services, and adopt those same marketing plans and methods to market or promote their business.

But, wait a minute. Who set up that system in the first place? And who says it's right or that it's the best system for you to use? The fact is that there are an unlimited number of methods of attracting new customers to your business, and your imagination is the only limiting factor.

Some of the best, most productive and cost-effective methods you can use can be adapted from what others are doing in totally unrelated businesses.

Now, this brings up a couple of questions. First, how observant are you? What are others in the same business doing? And, how effective are they?

Next, look around at what other unrelated businesses or professions are doing. Have you seen what's working for them? Is there one business that just stands out by doing something different or unusual? Or, do they all pretty much use the same marketing methods?

Next question: How creative are you? Can you look at what some of the other businesses are doing and adapt their methods to your business?

In other words, if you were brand new, just starting in business, and had no idea of what anyone before you had done to attract new customers, what would you do? How would you go about getting new customers? Would you use the same methods you use now, or would you do something completely different?

Romancing a New Client

Jim: *"After 10 years in the hotel business, I changed careers and decided to go to Wall Street. (That's a whole other story) As a new broker at Shearson Lehman in Beverly Hills, I attended my first sales meeting as a full fledged stock broker. After the manager made announcements and gave the stock recommendations for the day, the floor was open for discussion. As a new broker I had no clients and I naively asked "Who is the largest investor in the state of California?" Amid wry smiles and snickers, someone answered "The Los Angeles Police and Firemen's Pension Fund." Seasoned veterans looked at me with an attitude of "you poor child..." In spite of that I asked if anyone knew who the decision maker was. His name was Mike Bulpish but they all assured me he would not take on any new brokers. His Pension Fund had been doing business with our competition for years and wouldn't even consider changing companies.*

The next day, while all the other brokers were sitting at their desks, I located Mr. Bulpish's office and I drove into downtown LA and went to Little Joe's Italian Restaurant, ½ block from his office.

I waited until 12:05, hoping his secretary would be gone to lunch, and then I called his office. I was shocked when he answered. He was supposed to be so untouchable. I introduced myself and asked if he could join me for lunch right then and he said "Yes."(It would have been so easy to say to myself "He won't want to go or he's to busy or he already has plans" and then not call. I learned a lesson that day myself. Don't ever assume)

Mike Bulpish met me at Little Joe's and for the next 1 ½ hr. I listened enthusiastically. I asked him how he got in the business and what he did when he wasn't working. It came out that he graduated from Loyola High School and that his favorite collegiate team was Stanford.

I proceeded to tell him that my nephew was the all-CIF tail back for Loyola and he excitedly said "I love that kid! He's a real student athlete!" That little piece of information acted as glue for our first meeting and our conversation continued effortlessly.

Even though he told me that he couldn't give me any business because, by mandate, he had to use a company in the city of Los Angeles,(and we were in Beverly Hills), I still fed his passion which was Stanford football. I sent him the Sunday sports sections from the two San Francisco newspapers for the next two years.

Eventually Shearson opened an office just outside

Beverly Hills with a Los Angeles address. I moved to that office and sent Mike an announcement regarding my new location. Shortly after, my secretary Edna came rushing into my office and said "You won't believe what's happening!" We were receiving orders in 6 figure numbers to purchase stocks for the Pension Fund – all because I acknowledged his passion and found a way to help him enjoy it. When he received those newspapers in the mail, I can guarantee you that he was smiling as he was thinking of me because I was thinking of him. They were my client until I left the business.

So, what about you and your business? Specifically, what marketing methods are you using, *right now* to attract new customers and to build lasting relationships with them so they'll do business with you for a lifetime?

And how many *different* marketing methods do you presently and concurrently have working for you? There's a real danger in having just one or two main methods of attracting new customers.

One of our consulting clients depended almost entirely on a telemarketing team to acquire leads for their salespeople to follow up with. When a well-funded competitor opened for business nearby, they hired nearly all that business' telemarketing staff and nearly shut the business down.

When they called us in as consultants, we could see that we had to do something quick, just to save the business. So we got to work and hired and trained a whole new telemarketing crew and got the business up and running again.

But then we looked at other marketing options and put together an effective direct-mail program, started a proactive referral-generating system, and worked out some joint ventures and host-beneficiary relationships with other, complementary, but non-competing businesses.

Now, if something happens to any one of their marketing methods, they have other strategies or other "pillars" in place that can keep the business from collapsing and keep it running smoothly.

How can you apply this in your business?

Make sure you're not dependent on only one or two main methods of attracting new customers. It's critical that you have multiple systems in place to ensure that your business continues running, *and growing,* uninterrupted, if anything unexpected happens.

New customers are absolutely vital, not only to the growth of your business, but to the very survival of the business.

Because of the limited amount of space in these pages, we can't talk about all the methods of getting new customers, but in the training materials and workshops we conduct, we go into great detail on effective ways to attract prospects by the bushel, and convert them into loyal, long-term customers.

As important as it is to get more new customers, there are still three more methods you can use to grow your business. And each of these methods is more profitable and more effective, and gives you greater potential for leverage than the first method.

Let's talk about number two…

2. Get Your Customers to Make Larger Average Purchases

Simply put, get them to spend more money when they buy something from you.

This just happens to be the quickest and easiest way to increase your profits. It is amazing the number of businesses that have *extensive* and *expensive* plans in place to acquire more customers. Yet, very few have paid much attention to this highly profitable step of increasing the size of the order - getting more money from each of your customers every time they buy from you.

If you think for a minute about how easy this is and how profitable it can be, you'll see why it's such a powerful concept. You'll also see why nearly every fast-food restaurant has embraced, and mastered this concept; why they require that every person who takes orders must understand and be proficient in the use of the "up-sell" and "cross-selling" principles.

Think back about your own fast-food restaurant experience. You drive up to the speaker and place your order for a sandwich and a drink. Then what happens? A voice comes back over the speaker and asks if you'd like fries or an apple pie with your order.

That's an example of cross-selling which is

selling a product in addition to or beyond the initial purchase.

Or, they might suggest that you "super-size" your order. That's an example of up-selling or increasing the size of the initial order.

In any case, if you take them up on their suggestion, what they've done is just increase their profits *substantially*, since they made an additional sale, but had no acquisition or marketing costs.

They realize that a certain percentage of their customers will say, "yes" and the only reason they say "yes" is because a suggestion was made to them. So they play the numbers game.

And the result? Well, by being aware of what their customers might want but not ask for on their own, and then by asking questions or making suggestions, they bring in a substantial number of dollars. And other than the actual cost of the product, those dollars are pure profit.

Bundling is another marketing technique.

This is the technique where they combine a sandwich, a drink and fries, then throw in a couple of bonus items, like a cookie and a toy. They put it all together in one package, and give it a name like "Happy Meal."

They'll charge you less for that package than what each of those items purchased separately would have cost. But you end up spending more with them than you might have, had they not had the bundling.

Now, what does that have to do with you and your business?

Well, you may not be in the fast food business but the same principles can still apply. Just answer this question: What additional products or services do you have that would be natural complements to what your customers initially/or already buy from you?

If you have the type of business that offers more than one product to your customers, you have a tremendous advantage to capitalize on the up-selling, cross-selling and bundling techniques.

Do these things seem like common sense to you? Well, they probably do. But it's surprising how few businesses make effective use of these three simple principles.

Think about it. In reality, you have an obligation to your customers, the people who trust you to provide them good quality products and services and who hand over their hard-earned money to you. Your obligation is to make sure they get the very best value, the best use and the most enjoyment from their original purchase.

And if you have additional items, either products or services, that can enhance their value, their use or their enjoyment, then your obligation is to see that they at least have the option of taking advantage of those items.

Again, it's playing the numbers game. Some will take advantage of your offer and some won't. But at least you will have given them the opportunity and you will have fulfilled your obligation to them.

If you are sincere in your efforts, they'll realize that you are really trying to help them get more value, more use, and more benefit from their decision and their purchase.

And they'll come back to do business with you again and will refer others to you as well.

Up-selling, cross-selling and bundling - these are only three of many immediate, profit-producing methods you can use to skyrocket your business to the next level.

If you do nothing more than find a way to incorporate these three techniques in your business (which you should be able to do within the next twenty-four hours), you'll blast your profits completely through the roof.

Think about it - increasing your sales and increasing your *profits* - without increasing your expenses. It's an exciting concept and it can add an *immediate* twenty, thirty, even forty percent or more *in pure profits* to your bottom line!

Now, let's move on to the third way to grow your business.

3. Get Your Customers to Buy From You More Often

In other words, increase the frequency of their purchases. Give them reasons to want to come back and to continue doing business with you. The longer your customers go between purchases from you, the more chance they have of buying from your competition.

"Out of sight, out of mind." You need to

constantly stay in front of your customers. You need to educate them, tell them about new products, new lines, special incentives, and other offers that might benefit them.

The idea is two-fold: first, to "lock" your customers in so they can't afford to do business with anyone else and secondly, to make it so attractive to do business with you, that they wouldn't even consider going anywhere else.

What you really want to do is lead your customers to the inescapable and undeniable conclusion: that they would have to be completely out of their minds to even consider doing business with anyone else but you, regardless of the selection of products or services you provide, the prices you charge, your location, or the relationship they may have with the business they're currently doing business with.

Here is an example of how this works: One of our clients owns a restaurant. For his business customers who like to take their clients to lunch, he offers a certain number of lunches for a pre-paid, discounted price.

By doing this, he "locks in" his customer, gets his money up-front, and makes it convenient for everyone. The customer simply signs the check, which includes the tip. No money changes hands during or after the lunch, and new customers are constantly being introduced to his restaurant. As a result, many of those new customers take advantage of the same arrangement for their clients.

Here's another example. A car wash offers a

special pre-paid, discounted card that's good for a certain number of car washes. It's a great deal because you save money and it's convenient.

When the card is filled, you get a free car wax. It's a good deal for the car wash too because they've gotten their money up front and have locked you out from the competition.

Now, let's apply this concept your business. What can you think of that you could do that will endear your customers to you? How can you lock them in, get them coming back more often, and even refer others to do business with you?

Nina: *"I mail out a printed newsletter to my customers and clients every month and because of its success, in 2007 I was selected as one of the top 6 marketers of the year out of 20,000 marketers world wide. It was a big honor because the other 19,994 I competed against were all direct response marketers as well.*

My newsletter is always low budget. Never 4-color. Sometimes I will print it on colored paper. But it's full of personality. There are pictures of Jim and me wherever he's speaking, of my husband who grew a crazy mustache, puzzles, and cartoons. And of course, I'm always talking about marketing and what's working.

My newsletter has spawned another division in my company to produce newsletters. I've even hired a former Jay Leno writer to ghost write a column from my dog.

Your customers lose 10% of their potential sales value every month you do not stay in touch with them. Newsletters are an easy way to stay in touch.

- Do you send postcards or have a website that keeps them informed of new items and promotions?
- Do you hold special "Customer Appreciation Sales" or events?
- How about a frequent buyer club for your more loyal customers?
- What about a Referral Reward system that recognizes or compensates your customers for referring their friends?

You've got to let your customers know that you value and appreciate them, that you want them to come back, and that you want to make doing business with you fun, risk-free, rewarding,.

Well, you can see that the ideas are unlimited. While the restaurant and car wash examples may not apply directly to your business, they're included to serve as a stimulus. You can begin thinking of what you might consider applying in your business that can help you develop trust and loyalty with your customers.

In our coaching programs we go into great detail and discuss more than two-dozen very specific strategies that create an almost magnetic effect that keeps your customers returning time and time again.

We lead you by the hand and help you develop

personalized and effective strategies that keep them saying, "I'll be back"... strategies that keep them "insulated" from, and locked out of your competition.

Now let's talk about the fourth method you can use to grow your business. And that is to...

4. Extend Your Customers' "Average Buying Lifetime"

We call that "Customer Retention."

Here's what we mean: *How long, on average, do the people buy from you and remain your customers?*

In other words, how long do they continue doing business with you before they move on? Are they one-time buyers? Do they stay with you for a year, five years or ten years? Have you ever stopped to figure it out?

Next, what are you doing in your business *right now,* to make sure your customers *continue* doing business with you? If you don't have a strategic plan, a *working system* in place, you are going to lose a certain percentage of your current customers to the competition.

There's no question about it. Your competition... right now... *right this very minute* is making plans and taking steps to take your customers away from you.

The question for you is not, "What are you going to do about it?"

The *real* question is, "What are you *currently* doing about it?"

"What are you doing about it *right now?*"

What plans, what *systems* do you have in place

to keep your customers from defecting to the competition?

Let's talk about your customers for a minute. Are they *thrilled* enough with the products you offer and the services they receive from you to continue doing business with you year after year?

What if you answered "yes" to that question? The next questions would be, "Are you sure?"

"How do you know?"

"Where did you get your information?"

"How reliable is it?"

"Can you explain in detail, the *system* you have in place for finding out?"

Take note: "Are they *thrilled* enough?" Not "are they *satisfied* enough?" You see, there's a big difference between being *thrilled* and being *satisfied*.

Sixty percent of so-called "satisfied" customers switch companies or brands on a regular basis. We see it all the time with the utility companies. The phone companies, cable companies and energy companies are constantly trying to woo away their competitors' customers.

As a business owner, you can't afford not to thrill your customers. The cost is too high and unfortunately, most business owners simply don't understand this. Let's take a look at what the potential cost could mean to you if you fail to do these things.

Let's say that you make $200 in sales per year from your average customer.

And let's say that for any number of reasons, 100 customers stop doing business with you each year. They may die or move away. They may no longer need your products or services; they may switch companies, have a relative in the business, or possibly have a bad experience with someone in your company.

Or, they may just simply disagree with some policy or procedure you might have. It could be a falling out with a staff member or employee, a personality conflict, miscommunication, a problem they had with one of your products, or perhaps a feeling of neglect from you or someone in your business. It really doesn't matter what the reason is; they just stop doing business with you.

Well, those 100 customers no longer paying you $200 this year just cost you $20,000. But, that's not all. What if those 100 customers tell 5 others about their experience with you?

That's an additional 500 potential customers who won't be doing business with you this year (or maybe ever, for that matter).

And if each of them spent an average of $200, that's $100,000 you won't be receiving from them, PLUS the $20,000 you lost on your existing customers who left.

That brings the total in lost income to *$120,000 in just one year!*

It's not unusual for some businesses to bring in a hundred or more new customers each month. That's twelve hundred-plus customers a year, and they end up only netting a 150 or 200 increase at year-end (sometimes not even that).

Well, what happened to the other more than 1,000 customers? Where did they go? Surely, they all didn't die or move away.

But, you know, most business owners don't concern themselves with what or whom they've lost. They just focus on their net gain. They figure that if they finish the year with more customers or more sales than they started with, they're ahead.

Now, let's suppose that you gave those 100 lost customers reasons - good, compelling, life or business enhancing reasons - to continue doing business with you this year.

And let's suppose each of them told those same five people about their now-positive experience with you.

Well, there's $20,000 you wouldn't have lost in the first place, and another $100,000 you may possibly pick up from their referrals or by their word of mouth.

The point is, customers are important – *all* customers. In fact, they're critical. A business cannot remain in business unless it has someone to buy its products and services.

Those "someones" are people - real people, like you and like me. If you sell your products to the business community, remember, businesses don't buy from businesses.

People in business buy from other people in business. It's people that you market to. Not businesses.

Here's an interesting point: Most business

owners know exactly how much they have tied up in furniture, fixtures and equipment. They can tell you nearly to the penny how much each item cost, how old it is, how much it's depreciated and what the remaining life expectancy is.

That's important information for any business to have. But what's amazing is that very few business owners have any idea of what the value of their most important asset is… their customers.

Take a minute to think about how this whole concept relates to your business. What is it that you can do, *specifically,* to extend your customer's buying lifetime with you? Why not take a few minutes and answer these questions?

First of all, who are your customers … those who are buying from you now?

Who are their family members? Do you know the names of their spouse and/or children?

What are their hobbies or interests? What school do their children attend?

Do you know why they purchased a certain type of product or service?

Do you know who their friends, neighbors or relatives are?

What about your staff or employees? Do you know how they treat or feel about your customers? Do they, or do you, have favorite customers? What makes them a *"favorite?"* Is it how much they spend? How often they come in? Their personality? Do you treat those customers any different than the others?

Do you have regular staff meetings and talk about

how to think like a customer?

For example, have you thought about what you would want if you were: 1) A prospect considering doing business with you for the first time 2) An existing customer considering giving repeat business to your establishment or organization 3) An existing customer considering referring a friend, a family member or an acquaintance?

Do you have a training system in place to teach your staff how to handle or deal with difficult customers? Short-tempered customers? Analytical customers?

When a customer stops doing business with you, do you know why? Do you have a system in place to find out?

What would you have to do differently to get your customers to buy from you for 5½ years, instead of just 5 years?

If you will actually take the time to answer these questions and incorporate that information into your business practices, you can work wonders towards extending the buying lifetime of your customers. And as a result, you'll add *significant* profits to your bottom line.

We've covered a lot of ground and a lot of ideas so far. So let's pause for a minute and recap what we've discussed up to this point. There are four primary ways to grow a business.

1. **Get more customers.** And as mentioned, this is a vital step, but it's also the most difficult and the most costly.

2. **Get your customers to spend more money with you.** Increase the average transactional value of each sale. And remember, that this is the fastest and the easiest way to add immediate profits to your bottom line. (Remember the "bundling" concept.)
3. **Get your customers coming back to buy from you more often.** Keep your name in front of your customers. Don't let them forget you.
4. **Extend your customers' buying lifetime.** Find ways to retain them. Keep them as customers and keep them coming back as long as you possibly can.

It's really pretty simple. Nearly everything you do to build and grow your business falls under one of these four categories. There are more than two-dozen ways to apply these concepts and build your business, but for now, if you'll work on these four primary methods, you'll absolutely run circles around your competitors.

As you take a good, close-up look at these four areas, you'll see that what it really boils down to is effectively marketing your business. In other words, the success of your business enterprise depends largely on how effective your marketing system is.

That means that if you want your business to excel - really excel - if you want to virtually eliminate your competition and become the dominating force in your marketplace, then you've got to begin thinking of yourself as being in the *marketing* business, not in the product or service selling business.

In effect, you need to consider yourself as the head of a marketing organization that sells the products and services that your business offers.

Once you begin operating effectively in this capacity, you'll find that your job becomes much easier and much more enjoyable. Your prospects and customers will begin seeking you out and referring others to you, rather than you chasing after them. The net result will be that your marketing costs will plummet, and your profits will skyrocket!

"Only a life lived for others is a life worthwhile."
Albert Einstein

How Much Are Your Customers Really Worth?

Determining the Lifetime Profit Value of Your Customers

There's not much debate about this fact: Your existing customers or clients are your most valuable assets. The question is how much are they worth?

How much money, how much *profit* will you realize from each of your customers over their "buying lifetime" with you?

This is such an important concept that just knowing and understanding this one thing can have a bigger impact on your business than just about anything else you can do.

Once you understand it, a whole new set of factors will come into play and can absolutely revolutionize the way you look at your business, the way you *do* business, and the profits you'll generate as a result. To illustrate, here is an example.

Let's say that your average sale is $50. And let's say that your average customer buys from you 4 times per year.

So from those four transactions, you realize $200 in income. Let's say that this customer does business with you on average for 10 years. Over that 10-year period, or their "lifetime" of doing business with you, that average customer has been worth $2,000 in income to you.

Now, let's expand this example to a theoretical base of 1,000 customers and see what it means. Those 1,000 customers at $200 a year nets you an annual income of $200,000.

Let's assume that with the proper programs in place, you're able to increase each of the 4 ways to grow your business that we discussed earlier, by only 10 percent. Here's what happens:

First, the number of customers you have increases from 1,000 to 1,100.

Next, the average transaction amount per sale increases from $50 to $55.

Third, the average number of purchases per customer increases from 4 times to 4.4 times.

So, the annual income from your customer base will increase from $200,000 ($50 x 4 transactions x 1,000 customers) to $266,200 ($55 x 4.4 x 1,100 customers). That's an increase of $66,200 a year!

That's a huge increase!

But if you think that's exciting, wait till you see what happens if you were to extend your customer's buying lifetime by just 10 percent.

Let's say that your customers stay with you for 10 years, on average. Your lifetime value from those customers over that period of time would normally be $2,000,000. But, if you can extend that 10 years by just 10 percent to 11 years, your total dollar value from these customers will increase from $2,000,000 to $2,928,200 ($266,200 x 11 years)!

An increase of $928,200... nearly a million dollars! That's a *major* increase!

But that's not all. Let's say that you put an effective referral generating system in place, and that just 10 percent of your 1,000 customers send you a referral with a buying profile the same as your average customer.

That's an additional 100 customers who will bring you income of another $266,200 over the 11 years ($55 x 4.4 renewals x 100 customers x 11 years).

Total it all up, and you just made an additional $1,194,400! That's an average of $1,085,818 per year over the 11 years! Sound impossible? Well, it's not. And it's not all that difficult either. It can be done by simply increasing each of the four areas by only 10 percent!

Now, how hard would that be to do in your business? Could you realistically, and with some help, increase each of the four areas we discussed, by ten percent? What about twenty percent?

Some of the businesses we consult with, after realizing the power of this key concept and the others that we've discussed, have increased their businesses by as much as a hundred percent, or more in less than a year.

Maybe the numbers and figures we've discussed are realistic for you and your business and maybe they're not. Maybe you can't increase each of the areas by the same percentage. That's okay. That doesn't matter.

The point is you probably have room for improvement in one or more of the four areas. If you want your business to be a viable force in the marketplace, and to give you the lifestyle, the satisfaction and the income you want, you're going to have to take some proactive steps.

Knowing the Value of Your Customers Influences the Way You Treat Them

As mentioned before, just knowing how much your customers are worth to you can be invaluable and can help you in several ways.

First of all, we know that people don't do business with the same company or business forever. They stop doing business or change whom they do business with for a variety of reasons, and we've already discussed some of those.

However, if you just know, for instance, that your typical customer stays with you for ten years on average, that they're not just a one or two-time sale, you may begin to treat them differently.

You may give them some form of special treatment and you may even invite them to special, invitation-only, preferred customer seminars or events.

In other words, once you begin to see your customers in a different light, you may begin to do things differently in order to get them to stay longer as customers.

Next, if you know what the Lifetime Profit Value of your customers is, you'll probably discover that you can spend far more to acquire a new customer than you originally thought.

In other words, if your average customer is worth $2,000 in income to you, you can, theoretically, afford to spend up to $2,000 to bring in a new customer and still break even.

In theory, you could spend that $2,000 and still make a profit on the other "back end" products that you might be able to sell them.

And, if you put an effective referral-generating program in place, you can spend that same $2,000, and make your profits on the referrals they generate.

Of course it's unrealistic to think that you can really afford to spend the full amount of your lifetime income (in this case, $2,000), to get each new customer.

In reality, you've got to be concerned about things like overhead, cash-flow and reserves. You can't spend money you don't have.

Knowing the Value of Your Customers Influences How Much You Can Spend To Get a New One or Keep an Existing One

It comes down to two questions: How much can you *afford* to spend, and how much are you *willing* to spend to attract new business?

You may find that you can and are willing to spend five times what your competitors spend. And if they can't keep up with you, your business may just explode and leave them in the dust.

Just knowing you *margins* and that you could spend up to $2,000 and still break even, gives you a *tremendous* edge over your competition.

Here's a real-life example: Suppose you have a favorite restaurant you and your significant other like to go to about twice a month and your meals typically come to about $30. So $30 times 24 meals adds up to $720 in gross sales for the year.

Let's suppose that you continue to patronize that restaurant for10 years. That is your buying lifetime with that particular restaurant. That gives the restaurant a total of $7,200 in sales.

If over that 10-year period, you refer 10 people, 5 of whom become regular customers who have spending patterns similar to yours, they'll spend an additional $36,000. (That's 5 people, times $7200 a year.)

Add that to the $7,200 that you spent and you have been responsible for generating $43,200 for that restaurant. Even after deducting overhead expenses, the restaurant still realizes a healthy profit from the efforts of just one couple.

RESTAURANT EXAMPLE

A. Amount of average sale	$30
B. No. of sales/year/customer (2 x per month)	24
C. Gross income per year per customer (A x B)	$720
D. No. of years customer patronizes restaurant	10
E. Gross income over buying lifetime (C x D)	$ 7,200
F. No. of referrals from customer over buying lifetime	10
G. % of referrals who become a customer	50 %
H. Referrals who become customers (F xG)	5
I. Gross income from referrals (E x H)	$36,000
J. **Total value of a loyal customer (E + I)**	**$43,200**

Now, here's a question: Could that restaurant afford to give away a free meal to attract a new customer? Keep in mind that two of you are spending $30, so one meal costs $15, and out of that, about a third of it, or $5.00, is profit.

So, the meal really only costs the restaurant $10 and only part of that $10 goes to cover the cost of the food. The rest of the expense is in overhead, which would have to be paid whether or not a meal was served.

Of course the answer is *yes*. They *can* afford to give away a free meal. Not only that, they can afford to do many other things to not only attract new customers, but more importantly, make their existing customers feel more appreciated. And you know that when someone feels noticed, important, and appreciated, it's just natural that they'll want to return.

Let's imagine that you are a long-time, faithful customer of a certain restaurant and you brought your family, your clients or your business associates with you to eat there on a regular basis.

How would *you* feel if the manager were to offer you and your party a free dessert as a special appreciation gift for your loyalty and for the extra business you brought them? Do you think that little display of appreciation would cause you to want to return again?

And what about your guests? Do you think they would want to go back to that restaurant? Of course. And what about the restaurant's hard costs of those desserts - do you think the restaurant would lose any money on that gesture?

Not likely. You see, once you know how much profit your customers are worth to you long term, then and only then, can you determine how much you can afford to give away or spend to get new customers, or to keep your existing customers coming back. And you can begin to experiment with different offers to see which ones work best.

Suppose the owner of that restaurant spends $1000 on an ad or mailing to attract new customers. Two couples come in for dinner, and each spends $30.

Well, he's taken in a total of $60. But the ad costs were $1,000.

Does he consider the ad or mail campaign a loser and stop running it? That's what most business people do.

What would you do? Well, if you understand the concept of Lifetime Profit Value and Marginal Net Worth, you'll probably think differently.

When you consider the Lifetime Value of those customers, it changes the picture. With the proper care and attention, those customers could be responsible for $43,200 each, or $86,400 for the two of them.

Of course, those numbers are gross revenue figures, and you have to deduct for expenses. And it's over a 10-year period. Still, that represents a significant amount of money, and all from a $1,000 ad - an ad that most business owners would have given up on.

This is not to suggest that you have to settle for and be happy with low response rates for your ads. Certainly, you don't. You should always try to improve your ads, your letters, and your offers and give good, compelling reasons and benefits for someone to do business with you.

That's an entire subject in itself, and one we don't have time to discuss in great detail here. But it is one we take very seriously, and spend considerable time on in our workshops and coaching programs.

Let's go back and think about our restaurant example for a minute. Supermarkets and department stores use their own adaptation of this technique all the time. You've probably heard it referred to as a "loss leader."

What they do is advertise a few products at or below cost to bring new customers into their store, knowing that the customer will usually buy more products once they're in the store.

They also know that unless they get someone to visit their store in the first place, they could never stand a chance of making additional or repeat sales, or getting referrals from them. And additional and repeat sales to existing customers are generally easier to make and usually always bring higher profit margins.

Just remember this important point:

The first sale means nothing unless you're planning on going out of business next week. You've got to consider the Lifetime Profit Value - what your customer is worth to you- if you really want to be successful.

Now, how can you apply this concept of Lifetime Profit Value in your business?

Well, the first thing you can do is determine what the amount of your average income per sale is. The Lifetime Profit Value Calculator is provided for you to use in calculating the Lifetime Profit Value of your own customers. Fill out with your current figures to get an idea of how much your customers are worth to you.

The LPV Of Your Customers (Actual)

A. Amount of average sale	$
B. No. of sales/year/customer (2 x per month)	
C. Gross income per year per customer (A x B)	$
D. No. of years customer patronizes your business	
E. Gross income over buying lifetime (C x D)	$
F. No. of referrals from customer over buying lifetime	
G. % of referrals who become a customer	%
H. Referrals who become customers (F x G)	
I. Gross income from referrals (E x H)	$
J. Total value of a loyal customer (E + I)	$

This next calculator is provided so you can calculate what kind of a difference it will make to your business if you increased each of the areas by 10 percent.

Keep in mind as you do these calculations that this is a very simplified calculation. In our consulting sessions we get very detailed and take into consideration many more areas. So the results you'll see in actuality will be dramatically increased. But for an easy – to - demonstrate way to determine your customers' value to you, these basic calculators will do quite nicely.

The LPV Of Your Customers (+10%)

A. Amount of average sale	$
B. No. of sales/year/customer (2 x per month)	
C. Gross income per year per customer (A x B)	$
D. No. of years customer patronizes your business	
E. Gross income over buying lifetime (C x D)	$
F. No. of referrals from customer over buying lifetime	
G. % of referrals who become a customer	%
H. Referrals who become customers (F x G)	
I. Gross income from referrals (E x H)	$
J. Total value of a loyal customer (E + I)	$

"It's not what happens to you in life, but what you do about it that matters."
Jim Connelly

EPILOGUE

Where Do You Go From Here?

Congratulations for making it this far. You have now been exposed to some of the most powerful and effective techniques, concepts and ideas available for succeeding in business.

But no matter how good these ideas are, just being exposed to them is not enough. You must do something with them. In order for you to get the most value out of this material, you might want to consider developing a step by step action plan. An effective and results producing plan should consist of 5 areas:

1. EVALUATION

Ideas are nothing more than ideas until they are put into action. Once acted on, they have the potential to literally turn around a struggling business, or help an already successful business become even more dynamic and successful.

But before a person runs out and implements a new found idea, they should first take the time to evaluate their operation to determine just what areas are most lacking and could use the most attention.

You have the potential of making the most improvement in your own business if you will first take the time to identify and work on the area of greatest need.

2. RESEARCH

Once you've identified your greatest needs and placed them in priority order, you can begin to search out available solutions. Be on an opportunity lookout. The material in this book is just the beginning of the many places you can find good, usable, and practical ideas.

Don't turn any ideas away just because you think they might not pertain to your business or the way you operate. Capture them and then apply step number three.

3. PERSONALIZATION

As you encounter new ideas, keep an open mind. Study them. Analyze them. Think them through. Ask yourself if an application can be made to your specific situation by simply changing or modifying part of the concept or idea.

If a certain illustration uses a certain type of product or service for the example, but you don't sell that product or service, a simple adjustment might be all that's needed.

The material in this book is designed to illustrate concepts and only uses certain types of products as examples to make various points.

4. IMPLEMENTATION

Just as a membership in a health club won't do you any good unless you go there and use it, so too, is the information in this book.

It is of no practical use unless it is implemented. It's easy to come up with good ideas and develop plans, but where most people get bogged down is when it comes to putting them into action. It's not always easy, but if you're going to truly be successful, you must do whatever it takes to act on your plans. You must develop a Plan of Action.

5. REVIEW

After you've worked with your new ideas for a period of time, stop and evaluate how things are working. You may need to make some adjustments so you can continue to see improvement.

Some¬times an idea you thought was great, doesn't work out at all. That's okay. Stop using it. Just scrap it and move on to something else.

On the other hand, if you find an idea that works well, see if you can refine it, or "plus" it to make it even more effective.

The plain and truthful facts are that most people simply won't take the time and effort to do the things we've just discussed. On one hand, that's unfortunate because they could be even more successful than they are now.

On the other hand, their failure to take action is good for you because if it's you who does these things and not them, it will be you who realizes the success.

Now you have the tools…

GO FOR IT!

Above: Jim's first office—under the bridge in Turtle Creek. Below: Jim's second office – The Beverly Wilshire Hotel

Jim's third office—Marina City Club in Marina del Rey

Jim escorts John F. Kennedy on the campaign trail in California

Left: Jim spends a moment with Jerome Bettis while Lou Holtz looks on. Below: Jim celebrates with Wayne Gretzky after winning the Stanley Cup.

Above: Jim and his good friend, Rocky Bleier.

Right: Jim and his wife, Kate, with President Bush

Left: Jim and Nina with their scholarship recipient, Eric

Below: Nina with Lou Holtz

Left: Nina dresses up for her October newsletter picture.

*Top: Jim and his son, Jeff, with Dick Notebaert,
Chairman of the Notre Dame Board of Trustees.
Center left: Rudy and Jim standing in the Notre Dame
stadium where Rudy caught the famous touchdown.
Center Right: Rudy with Jim's daughter, Katy Clare.*

Above: Lifelong friends Ralph, Jim Donna, Richie, and Jack. Below: Jim with his mother and Joe Montana.

Above: Jim and Lou Holtz during Lou's college Hall of Fame induction in New York.

Left: Jim and Nina before Jim's keynote speech for the Napoleon Hill Foundation's annual event.

Below: Jim with Lou Holtz and Mike Leep.

Top: Our January 2009 MasterMind Group
From Left to right: Drew, Isaac, Jim, Becky, Jim, Andy,
Lucy, John, Magesh, Carole, Marlene, Laura, Nina

Below: Jim on Air Force One

Share These Books With Others

Want to share this book with others? **$19.95 single copy**

SPECIAL QUANTITY DISCOUNTS

2-20 Books................. $15.00 each
21-99 Books................ $14.00 each
100 – 499 Books......... $13.00 each
500 – 999 Books......... $12.00 each
1,000 + Books............. $10.00 each

One More Sunset **is an extraordinary account of Donna Jones's brush with death and her courageous fight to live. *$15 single copy*.**

SPECIAL QUANTITY DISCOUNTS

2-20 Books................... $10.00 each
21-99 Books................. $9.00 each
100 – 499 Books........... $8.00 each
500 – 999 Books........... $7.00 each
1,000 + Books.............. $6.00 each

To place an order, visit www.Jim-Connelly.com
or call 574-320-2522

Other Resources

Business Coin

No marketing piece you've ever seen is as powerful as Jim Connelly's coin. He hears stories daily of it being their motivational "magic coin" or how they have it in their pocket or on their desk as a reminder to "Think Like a Champion".

Size: 1.75" and 3 mm thick.
$49 plus $3.50 s/h

Jim Connelly is available for speaking engagements. To check availability, call 574-320-2522

Lou Holtz Limited Edition Lithograph

With only 1,000 available for the world market, this limited edition full color lithograph celebrates the coaching genius of this legendary coach during his time as head coach at the University of Notre Dame.

Jim Connelly commissioned renowned artist Curt Sochocki to commemorate Lou's "100 Wins." A portion of the money raised through the sale of these lithographs goes to support nursing scholarships in honor of Lou's mother, Anne.

All lithographs come with a certificate of authenticity and are signed and numbered by the artist. **$150** (includes insured shipping costs)

Lithographs signed by the Coach himself (includes insured shipping costs) **$350**

"The Best of Jim Connelly"

Have the master mentor himself teach you his most powerful secrets of his extraordinary success. This 8 CD audio set includes

- Jim's live presentation of *"Feel the Fear and Do it Anyway"*,
- An interview with the Napoleon Hill Foundation about the influence of *"Think and Grow Rich"* in his life
- And 6 other audios about

  Romancing the Customer – *how to turbo-charge your client relationships for maximum lifelong business*

  Developing Centers of Influence – create million dollar habits that will grow your bottom line profits

  The Mentoring Factor – how to find the right mentor to help you develop a visionary mindset with clearly defined goals

  Thick Skin – thrive in any economy and in any environment by developing your own unwavering focus

  The Power of a Simple Thank You – Uncommon handwritten notes create unforgettable relationships

  How Winners Become Champions - Move away from the pack and stand *alone at the top*

Tax Deductable Investment: $397

Speaking Engagements

In addition to being a Business Development Expert, Jim Connelly also travels worldwide inspiring and motivating audiences to pursue their dreams and never give up. To check his speaking schedule, call 248-756-6314 or email him at jcnd@comcast.net.

Jim was the keynote speaker for the Napoleon Hill Foundation's annual event.

Jim,

It has only been three days since you spoke to the students and guests at the annual Napoleon Hill Day Celebration held annually on the University of Virginia's College at Wise Campus.

The response has been remarkable. Students, school administrators, and professors at the University have been lavish with their praise of your message.

Jim, while listening and watching the audience's responses, it was obvious that you succeeded beyond our wildest expectations. You made a difference!

Don Green,
Executive Director, The Napoleon Hill Foundation

CREATING CLIENTS FOR LIFE

SECRETS FOR LIFELONG RELATIONSHIPS

40 years after leaving the General Manager position from the Beverly Wilshire Hotel, Jim Connelly can walk in the hotel and still have people wanting to meet with him. For the first time ever he has partnered with internationally known marketer, Nina Hershberger to share both their secrets to lifelong relationships and clients for life.

JIM CONNELLY Jim Connelly was born and raised in the projects of Turtle Creek, Pennsylvania - a depressed factory town near Pittsburgh. His father was the town bully, an alcoholic who physically beat him on a regular basis. Life was not easy for the young Connelly and school did not rank high on his priority list. As a result, he couldn't spell, couldn't read, and couldn't do math that required a letter with the numbers. He failed his sophomore year becoming the only one in his high school required to go 5 years. In every area that society measures success, Jim was a failure. And yet against all odds at age 27 - 6 years after leaving Turtle Creek with $100 in his pocket - he was the General Manager of the Beverly Wilshire Hotel - one of the most prestigious hotels in Beverly Hills, California.

NINA HERSHBERGER is a nationally-recognized marketing whiz whose ideas and opinions have been featured on (and in) CNBC, CBS MoneyWatch.com, Market Watch, Forbes, The Wall Street Journal and many other news outlets. Once a purchasing agent at the University of Notre Dame, this out-of-the-box thinker is known world-wide as "The Wallet Mailer Lady" and was featured in Bill Glazer's bestselling book Outrageous Advertising. Nina's company, Megabucks Marketing, is a direct response brand developer. But don't get in her way. The only thing that matters for Nina is how much gets done at the end of the day. Good ideas never implemented are worthless.

ISBN $12.95

9 781484 854631

JIM CONNELLY & NINA HERSHBERGER